Environmental Lifestyle Guide

For Grade 9 Students

VOL.2 OF 11

ENERGY

Jahangir Asadi

Vancouver, BC CANADA

Published by: Silosa Consulting Group Inc.
Vancouver, BC **CANADA**
Email: Info@Silosa.ca
www.silosa.ca

Ordering Information:
Quantity sales. Special discounts are available on quantity purchases by universities, schools, corporations, associations, and others. For details, contact the "Sales Department" at the above mentioned email address.

Environmental lifestyle Guide Vol.2 for Grade.9/J.Asadi —1st ed.
ISBN: 978-1-990451-76-8

Contents

We hope that, 10,000 years from now, future generations will be able to see flowers that provide bees with nectar and pollen and...
BEES provide flowers with the means to reproduce by spreading pollen from flower to flower,....

Jahangir Asadi

This book is dedicated to my professor, Dr.Sadeq Fakhr

The more you care about our environment, the more it will be protected from contaminants and toxins

Introduction

This book is part of an eleven volume series that is meant to be a standard textbook series, for grades 9 to 12. TTAIN & ESFK & SCG improves quality of life and reduces environmental degradation by fostering new consumption patterns and sustainable lifestyles through International Cooperative Extension Service programs at houses, offices, schools and libraries all over the globe.

Climate change is real. Therefore people have the potential to make a difference now and for future generations. This book provides climate science basics, including the roles that lifestyles and populations play in the climate scenario, the significance of carbon footprints, and an overview of the current climate situation. The manual has been categorized based on humanity's needs starting first with food and ending with tourism. The manual then illustrates the difference between adaptation (taking steps to live with the changes) and mitigation (taking steps to slow the rate of change.)

Adaptation examples include food, energy, transportation, recreation. Mitigation focuses on effectively engaging with local governments, through serving on advisory boards, communicating with public officials, educational institutes, schools, universities, libraries and leading communities towards climate change actions.

One useful way to mitigate climate change is through increasing public knowledge to better understand the impact of the rate of change on plants and animals. This is crucial for preserving species; and for assessing potential insects and disease outbreaks in agriculture, natural resources and public health.

Taking personal action is a key element of this manual.

Citizens are challenged to consume 20% fewer resources, to bring world consumption levels down as much as possible. Readers are given 12 practical steps to take to make the changes. The resources section provides additional information, and readers are encouraged to contact the author for further questions.

As an accessibility action, we have provided Online international courses on climate change control as well. You can access the courses via the following link:

http://TopTenAward.org

SILOSA Consulting Group (SCG)

Silosa Consulting Group (SCG) was established to provide outstanding consulting services of management system & educational standards to individuals, groups, companies, schools, and organizations all over the globe. SCG is publishing an "Environmental Lifestyle Guide " book series as a standard textbook related to increasing environmental awareness of students means being aware of the natural environment and making choices that benefit the earth, rather than hurt it. Vol.1 to 11 (for grades 9 to 12) providing some of the ways to practice environmental awareness include: **Recycling**, **Conserving energy and water**, **Reuse, Activism, and others**.

SCG book publishing services and distribution services are connected to over 39,000 booksellers worldwide, including Apple, Amazon, Barnes & Noble, Indigo, Google Play Books, and many more. SCG has enough experiences to help create new and effective environmental educational programmes in different countries all over the world. For more detail, visit our website : http://silosa.ca and/or send your enquirer to the following email:

info@silosa.ca

CHAPTER 1

About ISO 14000 for Students

The International Organization for Standardization is an independent, non-governmental organization, the members of which are the standards organizations of the 165 member countries. It is the world's largest developer of voluntary international standards and it facilitates world trade by providing common standards among nations. More than twenty thousand standards have been set, covering everything from manufactured products and technology to food safety, agriculture, and healthcare.

Kids ISO 14000s
"Kids ISO 14000s" is a new environmental education program for children, based on ISO 14000s, which is international standard for environmental management. Primary aims of this program are: -
1. To teach and train children how to manage the environmental issues (such as energy saving) by themselves through the working book and guide book of this program,
2. To certify those children who showed good accomplishment in the program from highly international authority (as is the case of ISO 14000s)
3. To network those children through the international network (Kids International Network), so that the children can work on the environment, internationally.

2. System of Kids ISO 14000s Program
The system of Kids ISO 14000s Program consists of
1. Operation Headquarter (ArTech).
2. Workbook, Guidebook (originally published by ArTech, and local versions are produced by each countries).
3. Eco-Kids-Instructors for local operation and evaluation of the performance of the children.
4. International accreditation committee for accreditation of accomplishment of the children, for certification of the Eco-Kids-Instructors, as well as overall checks of this program.
5. Linkage with international organizations (such as UNU, UNESCO, etc. …) And also national organizations

More information can be obtained :

www.ISO.org

Canada

Environmental Sustain for Future kids established in Vancouver, BC Canada in 2020. (ESFK) is an international ecolabel focused on taking care of environment for future of kids. ESFK defined as 'self-declared' environmental claims made by manufacturers and businesses based on ISO 14020 series of standards, the claimant can declare the environmental objectives and targets in relation to taking care of environment for future kids. However, this declaration will be verifiable.

Environmental Sustain for Future Kids
Vancouver, BC CANADA

Email: info@esfk.org
Web: www.esfk.org

STEP TWO

What is Renewable energy ?

R enewable energy is energy that has been derived from earth's natural resources that are not finite or exhaustible, such as wind and sunlight. Renewable energy is an alternative to the traditional energy that relies on fossil fuels, and it tends to be much less harmful to the environment.

Types of Renewable Energy :

S olar energy is derived by capturing radiant energy from sunlight and converting it into heat, electricity, or hot water. Photovoltaic (PV) systems can convert direct sunlight into electricity through the use of solar cells.

Wind farms capture the energy of wind flow by using turbines and converting it into electricity. There are several forms of systems used to convert wind energy and each vary. Commercial grade wind-powered generating systems can power many different organizations, while single-wind turbines are used to help supplement pre-existing energy organizations.

Hydroelectric, Dams are what people most associate when it comes to hydroelectric power. Water flows through the dam's turbines to produce electricity, known as pumped-storage hydropower. Run-of-river hydropower uses a channel to funnel water through rather than powering it through a dam.

Geothermal heat is heat that is trapped beneath the earth's crust from the formation of the Earth 4.5 billion years ago and from radioactive decay. Sometimes large amounts of this heat escapes naturally, but all at once, resulting in familiar occurrences, such as volcanic eruptions and geysers.

Ocean, the ocean can produce two types of energy: thermal and mechanical. Ocean thermal energy relies on warm water surface temperatures to generate energy through a variety of different systems. Ocean mechanical energy uses the ebbs and flows of the tides to generate energy, which is created by the earth's rotation and gravity from the moon.

Hydrogen needs to be combined with other elements, such as oxygen to make water as it does not occur naturally as a gas on its own. When hydrogen is separated from another element it can be used for both fuel and electricity.

Bioenergy is a renewable energy derived from biomass. Biomass is organic matter that comes from recently living plants and organisms. Using wood in your fireplace is an example of biomass that most people are familiar with.

Renewable Energy: What Can You Do?

As a consumer you have several opportunities to make an impact on improving the environment through the choice of a greener energy solution. If you're a homeowner, you have the option of installing solar panels in your home. Solar panels not only reduce your energy costs, but help improve your standard of living with a safer, more eco-friendlier energy choice that doesn't depend on resources that harm the environment. There are also alternatives for a greener way of life offered by your electric companies. Just Energy allows consumers to choose green energy options that help you reduce your footprint with energy offsets.

Solar

Solar energy is derived by capturing radiant energy from sunlight and converting it into heat, electricity, or hot water. Photovoltaic (PV) systems can convert direct sunlight into electricity through the use of solar cells.

Benefits

One of the benefits of solar energy is that sunlight is functionally endless. With the technology to harvest it, there is a limitless supply of solar energy, meaning it could render fossil fuels obsolete. Relying on solar energy rather than fossil fuels also helps us improve public health and environmental conditions. In the long term, solar energy could also eliminate energy costs, and in the short term, reduce your energy bills. Many federal local, state, and federal governments also incentivize the investment in solar energy by providing rebates or tax credits.

Current Limitations

Although solar energy will save you money in the long run, it tends to be a significant upfront cost and is an unrealistic expenses for most households. For personal homes, homeowners also need to have the ample sunlight and space to arrange their solar panels, which limits who can realistically adopt this technology at the individual level.

Wind

Wind farms capture the energy of wind flow by using turbines and converting it into electricity. There are several forms of systems used to convert wind energy and each vary. Commercial grade wind-powered generating systems can power many different organizations, while single-wind turbines are used to help supplement pre-existing energy organizations. Another form is utility-scale wind farms, which are purchased by contract or wholesale. Technically, wind energy is a form of solar energy. The phenomenon we call "wind" is caused by the differences in temperature in the atmosphere combined with the rotation of Earth and the geography of the planet.

Benefits

Wind energy is a clean energy source, which means that it doesn't pollute the air like other forms of energy. Wind energy doesn't produce carbon dioxide, or release any harmful products that can cause environmental degradation or negatively affect human health like smog, acid rain, or other heat-trapping gases. Investment in wind energy technology can also open up new avenues for jobs and job training, as the turbines on farms need to be serviced and maintained to keep running.

Current Limitations

Since wind farms tend to be built in rural or remote areas, they are usually far from bustling cities where the electricity is needed most. Wind energy must be transported via transition lines, leading to higher costs. Although wind turbines produce very little pollution, some cities oppose them since they dominate skylines and generate noise. Wind turbines also threaten local wildlife like birds, which are sometimes killed by striking the arms of the turbine while flying.

Hydroelectric

Dams are what people most associate when it comes to hydroelectric power. Water flows through the dam's turbines to produce electricity, known as pumped-storage hydro power. Run-of-river hydro power uses a channel to funnel water through rather than powering it through a dam.

Benefits

Hydroelectric power is very versatile and can be generated using both large scale projects, like the Hoover Dam, and small scale projects like underwater turbines and lower dams on small rivers and streams. Hydroelectric power does not generate pollution, and therefore is a much more environmentally-friendly energy option for our environment.

Current Limitations

Most hydroelectricity facilities use more energy than they are able to produce for consumption. The storage systems may need to use fossil fuel to pump water. Although hydroelectric power does not pollute the air, it disrupts waterways and negatively affects the animals that live in them, changing water levels, currents, and migration paths for many fish and other freshwater ecosystems.

Geothermal

Geothermal heat is heat that is trapped beneath the earth's crust from the formation of the Earth 4.5 billion years ago and from radioactive decay. Sometimes large amounts of this heat escapes naturally, but all at once, resulting in familiar occurrences, such as volcanic eruptions and geysers. This heat can be captured and used to produce geothermal energy by using steam that comes from the heated water pumping below the surface, which then rises to the top and can be used to operate a turbine.

Benefits

Geothermal energy is not as common as other types of renewable energy sources, but it has a significant potential for energy supply. Since it can be built underground, it leaves very little footprint on land. Geothermal energy is naturally replenished and therefore does not run a risk of depleting (on a human timescale).

Current Limitations

Cost plays a major factor when it comes to disadvantages of geothermal energy. Not only is it costly to build the infrastructure, but another major concern is its vulnerability to earthquakes in certain regions of the world.

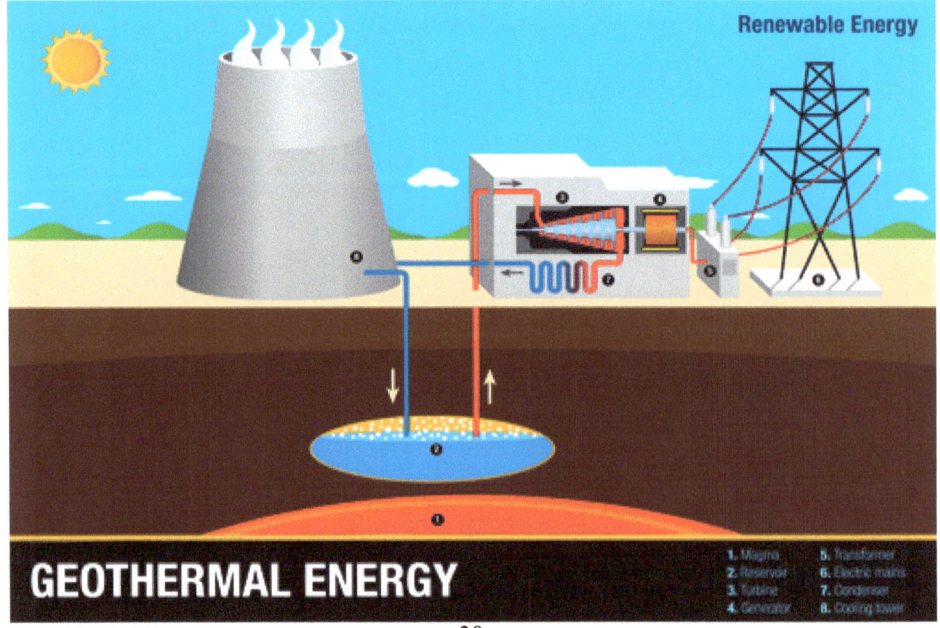

Ocean

The ocean can produce two types of energy: thermal and mechanical. Ocean thermal energy relies on warm water surface temperatures to generate energy through a variety of different systems. Ocean mechanical energy uses the ebbs and flows of the tides to generate energy, which is created by the earth's rotation and gravity from the moon.

Benefits

Unlike other forms of renewable energy, wave energy is predictable and it's easy to estimate the amount of energy that will be produced. Instead of relying on varying factors, such as sun and wind, wave energy is much more consistent. This type of renewable energy is also abundant, the most populated cities tend to be near oceans and harbors, making it easier to harness this energy for the local population. The potential of wave energy is an astounding as yet untapped energy resource with an estimated ability to produce 2640 TWh/yr. Just 1 TWh/yr of energy can power around 93,850 average U.S. homes with power annually, or about twice than the number of homes that currently exist in the U.S. at present.

Current Limitations

Those who live near the ocean definitely benefit from wave energy, but those who live in landlocked states won't have ready access to this energy. Another disadvantage to ocean energy is that it can disturb the ocean's many delicate ecosystems. Although it is a very clean source of energy, large machinery needs to be built nearby to help capture this form energy, which can cause disruptions to the ocean floor and the sea life that habitats it. Another factor to consider is weather, when rough weather occurs it changes the consistency of the waves, thus producing lower energy output when compared to normal waves without stormy weather.

Hydrogen
Hydrogen needs to be combined with other elements, such as oxygen to make water as it does not occur naturally as a gas on its own. When hydrogen is separated from another element it can be used for both fuel and electricity.

Benefits
Hydrogen can be used as a clean burning fuel, which leads to less pollution and a cleaner environment. It can also be used for fuel cells which are similar to batteries and can be used for powering an electric motor.

Current Limitations
Since hydrogen needs energy to be produced, it is inefficient when it comes to preventing pollution.

Biomass

Bioenergy is a renewable energy derived from biomass. Biomass is organic matter that comes from recently living plants and organisms. Using wood in your fireplace is an example of biomass that most people are familiar with.

There are various methods used to generate energy through the use of biomass. This can be done by burning biomass, or harnessing methane gas which is produced by the natural decomposition of organic materials in ponds or even landfills.

Benefits

The use of biomass in energy production creates carbon dioxide that is put into the air, but the regeneration of plants consumes the same amount of carbon dioxide, which is said to create a balanced atmosphere. Biomass can be used in a number of different ways in our daily lives, not only for personal use, but businesses as well. In 2017, energy from biomass made up about 5% of the total energy used in the U.S. This energy came from wood, biofuels like ethanol, and energy generated from methane captured from landfills or by burning municipal waste.

Current Limitations

Although new plants need carbon dioxide to grow, plants take time to grow. We also don't yet have widespread technology that can use biomass in lieu of fossil fuels.

The Future of Renewable energy

Take a moment to close your eyes and imagine the world ten, twenty, fifty years from now. How do you heat your home? What do our energy systems look like? How about our cars – how are they fueled?

In an ideal world, renewable energy will become the primary source of the planet's energy, as opposed to traditional energy sources, like fossil fuels (which release harmful carbon emissions and pollution into the atmosphere). So, what does the future of renewable energy actually look like? Time will tell – but these crazy, cool, new innovations may provide a glimpse into the future of renewables:

Solar Powered Panels that Chase the Sun

Genius in its simplicity, this new technology overcomes one of the biggest challenges facing solar power – clouds and inclement weather. These solar panels actually reposition themselves to soak in the most possible sunlight, resulting in much higher levels of efficiency.

Solar/Wind Hybrids

As solar and wind technologies continue to improve, scientists and engineers are experimenting with ways to make both more efficient. Bring on the superhero of renewable energy: solar and wind hybrids. This technology combines wind turbines with solar photovoltaic (PV) panels to produce higher levels of energy – and studies have found that they are nearly twice as efficient.

Energy From Unusual Sources

You've heard about energy from the wind, from the sun, and even from compost or other organic sources, but how about algae? It's true – "algae energy" is a concept that scientists are currently developing. Another awesome technology: these batteries made from wood (oh hey there, bioenergy). Color us impressed.

Do-It-Yourself Renewable Energy

We dream of a world with solar panels on every roof, wind turbines in every backyard. Is this a realistic dream? Scientists and engineers are getting closer every day. Even today, some dedicated homeowners have taken pains to install their own personal systems of solar power to heat/power their homes – a trend we hope to see continue well into the future.

Nuclear Energy Is Extraordinary

Nuclear energy comes from splitting atoms in a reactor to heat water into steam, turn a turbine and generate electricity. Ninety-four nuclear reactors in 28 states generate nearly 20 percent of the nation's electricity, all without carbon emissions because reactors use uranium, not fossil fuels. These plants are always on: well-operated to avoid interruptions and built to withstand extreme weather, supporting the grid 24/7.

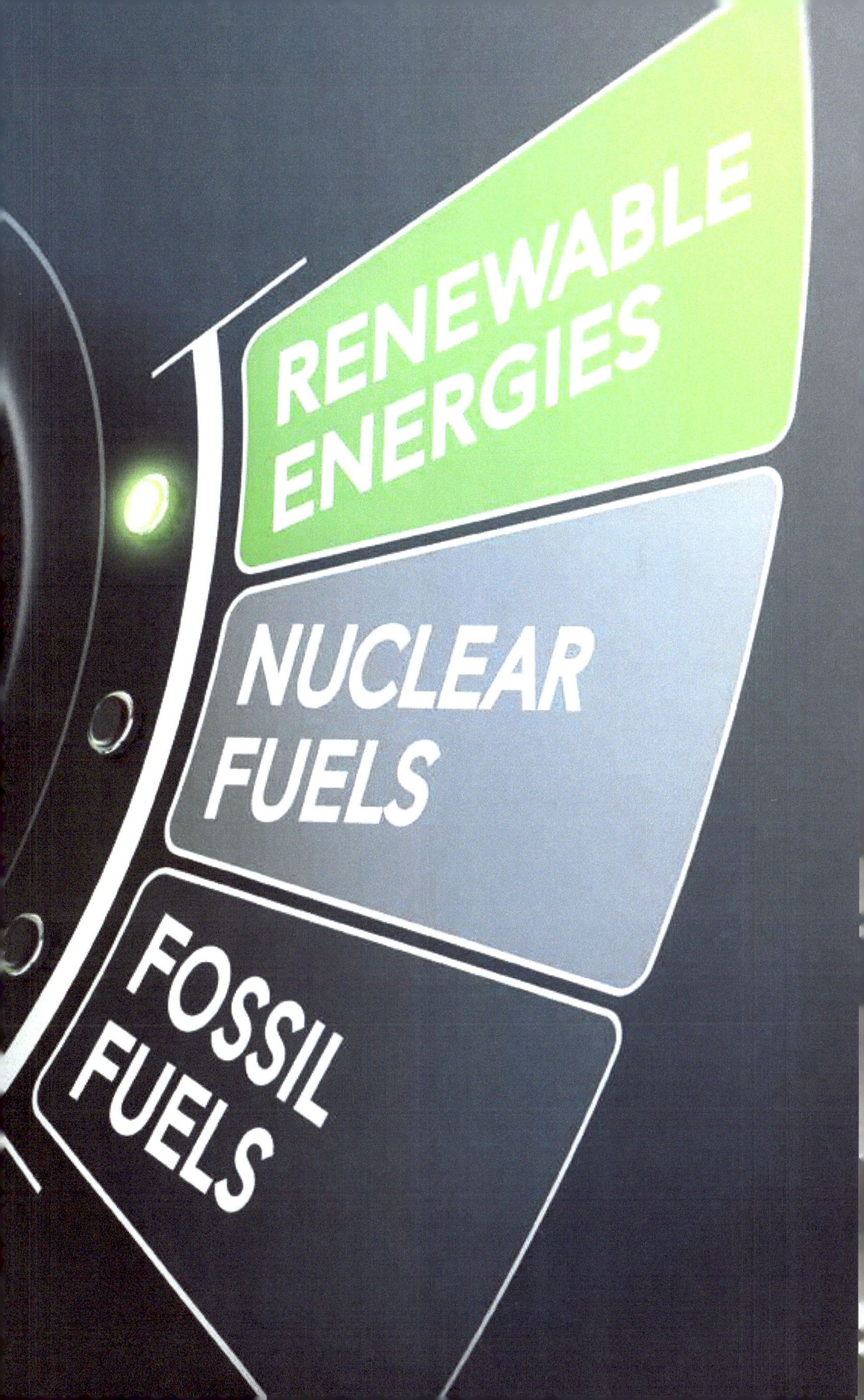
RENEWABLE
ENERGIES
NUCLEAR
FUELS
FOSSIL
FUELS

CANADA BRONZE BEAVER BADGE

Participate in our Online Classes to earn these exclusive digital badges!
www.toptenaward.org

Design & Development by:

Tara Asadi

1) ____ _____ is derived by capturing radiant energy from sunlight and converting.
A) Wind energy
B) Solar energy
C) Geothermal
D) Electric Energy
ANSWER:

2) Because of _____ _____In 2017, energy from biomass made up about %5 of the total energy used in the U.S.
A) Wind energy
B) Developed Equipment's
C) Geothermal
D) Current Limitations
ANSWER:

3) Hydroelectric power is very versatile and can be generated using both small scale projects, like the Hoover Dam, and small-scale projects like underwater turbines and lower dams on small rivers and streams.
A) True
B) False
ANSWER:

4) Correct Sentence: Hydroelectric power is very versatile and can be generated using both large scale projects, like the Hoover Dam, and small-scale projects like underwater turbines and lower dams on small rivers and streams.
A) True
B) False
ANSWER:

5) Formation of the _____ 4.5 billion years ago and from radioactive decay.

A) Lights   B) Sun
C) Earth   D) Moon

ANSWER:

6) Geothermal heat is heat that is trapped beneath the _____ ____.

A) Earth's Crust
B) River Base
A) Ocean's water
B) Sun Light

ANSWER:

7)_____ _____ is derived by capturing radiant energy from sunlight and converting it into heat, electricity, or hot water.

A) Earth's Crust
B) River Base
C) Solar Energy
D) Geo Magnetic

ANSWER:

8) Although new plants need carbon dioxide to grow, plants take _____ to grow.

A) one week
B) gas
C) food
D) Time

ANSWER:

9) When _____ is separated from another element it can be used for both fuel and electricity.

A) Hydrogen
B) oxygen
C) Nitrate
D) Alcohol

ANSWER:

10) We dream of a world with _____ _____ on every roof, wind turbines in every backyard.
A) Satellite Dish   B) Flags
C) Solar Panel   D) Vents
ANSWER:

11) Unlike other forms of _____ _____, wave energy is predictable and it's easy to estimate the amount of energy that will be produced.
A) Natural Gas
B) Crude Oil
C) Nuclear Power
D) Renewable Energy
ANSWER:

12) Technically, _____ _____ is a form of solar energy.
A) Natural Gas   B) Crude Oil
C) Wind Energy   D) Electric Energy
ANSWER:

13) _____ mechanical energy uses the ebbs and flows of the tides to generate.
A) Ocean   B) Nuclear
C) Wind   D) Geothermal
ANSWER:

14)_____ _____ is an alternative to the traditional energy that relies on fossil fuels, and it tends to be much less harmful to the environment.
A) Natural Gas   B) Crude Oil
C) Electric Energy   D) Renewable Energy
ANSWER:

15) With the technology to harvest it, there is a limitless supply of solar energy, meaning it could _____ _____ fuels obsolete.
A) Render fossil   B) Crude Oil
C) Animal Source   D) Renewable Energy
ANSWER:

16) Nuclear reactors in all over the world generate nearly 20 percent of the nation's electricity, all without carbon emissions because reactors use uranium, not fossil fuels, So its fully environmentally.
A) True
B) False
ANSWER:

17) One of the benefits of _____ _____ is that sunlight is functionally endless.
A) Natural Gas
B) Solar Energy
C) Electric Energy
D) Wind Energy
ANSWER:

18) Although _____ _____, it is a very clean source of energy, large machinery needs to be built nearby to help capture this form energy, which can cause disruptions to the ocean floor and the sea life that habitats it.
A) Natural Gas
B) Solar Energy
C) Ocean Energy
D) Wind Energy
ANSWER:

19) Space to arrange their _____ _____, which limits who can realistically adopt.
A) Electric Batteries   B) Solar Panels
C) Wind Turbines   D) Nuclear Plates
ANSWER:

20) _____ thermal energy relies on warm water surface temperatures to generate energy through a variety of different systems.
A) Natural   B) Solar
C) Ocean   D) Wind
ANSWER:

21) _____, Dams are what people most associate when it comes.
A) Hydroelectric
B) Hydro Power
C) Electricity Generation
D) Desalination
ANSWER:

22) Renewable energy is energy that has been derived from _____
natural resources that are not finite or exhaustible, such as wind and
sunlight.
A) Earth's
B) Solar
C) Ocean
D) Wind
ANSWER:

23) Since _____ needs energy to be produced, it is inefficient when it
comes.
A) Oxygen
B) Hydrogen
C) Electric
D) Gasoline
ANSWER:

24)There are several forms of systems used to convert wind energy
and each vary.
A) True
B) False
ANSWER:

25) The environmental problems directly related to energy production
and consumption include air pollution, climate change, water
pollution, thermal pollution, and solid waste disposal
A) True
B) False
ANSWER:

26) _____ thermal energy relies on warm water surface temperatures.
A) Earth's
B) Solar
C) Ocean
D) Wind
ANSWER:

27) In an ideal world, _____ _____ will become the primary source of.
A) Natural Gas
B) Renewable Energy
C) Electric Energy
D) Wind Energy
ANSWER:

28) _____ Energy is a clean energy source, which means that it doesn't pollute the air like other forms of energy.
A) Oil
B) Hydrogen
C) Gasoline
D) Wind
ANSWER:

29) If you're a homeowner, you have the option of installing _____ _____ in your home.
A) Electric Batteries
B) Solar Panels
C) Wind Turbines
D) Nuclear Plates
ANSWER:

30) If you will be out of a room for more than 15 minutes, turn off lights.
A) True
B) False
ANSWER:

CANADA SILVER BEAVER BADGE

Participate in our Online Classes to earn these exclusive digital badges!
www.toptenaward.org

Design & Development by:

Tara Asadi

Bibliography:

Andrews, R.N.L. 1998. Environmental regulation and business 'self-regulation'. Policy Sciences 31(3): 177-197.

Apodaca, Julia, "Market Potential of Organically Grown Cotton as a Niche Crop." Natural Fibers Research and Information Center, Bureau of Business Research, University of Texas at Austin, Paper presented at the Beltwide Cotton Conference in Nashville, TN, January 1992.

Asadi, J., "International Environmental Labelling, Economic Consequencies, Export Magazine, July 2001

Asadi, J. 2008. Mobile Phone as management systems tools, ISO Magazine, Vol.8, No.1

Asadi, J., Eco-Labelling Standards, National Standard Magazine, Sep. 2004.

Assocs., Cambridge MA and G. Davis, U. Tenn, Knoxville,TN. (68-W6-0021): xiii+76+226pp.

Balter, M. 1999. Scientific cross-claims fly in continuing beef war. Science (May 28) 284: 1453-1455.

Belsley, D.A., Kuh, E., and Welsch, R.E. (1980), Regression Diagnostics, New York: John Wiley & Sons, Inc.

Birett, M. J. 1997. Encouraging Green Procurement Practices in Business: A Canadian Case Study in Program Development (108-118). in Greener Purchasing : Opportunities and Innovation. Sheffield, Greenleaf Publishing 325p.

Bowen, Nicola, World Agrochemical Markets, PJB Publications Ltd., March 1991.

Bureau of Ocean Energy Management, Ocean Wave Energy, Retrieved From: https://www.boem.gov/Ocean-Wave-Energy/

Burnside, A., (1990), Keen on Green, Marketing, 17 May, pp35-36

Butler, D., (1990), A Deeper Shade of Green, Management Today, June, pp74-79

Cairncross, F. 1995. Green, Inc.: A guide to business and the environment. London, Earthscan. 277p.

Cason, T. N. and L. Gangadharan, (2002), Environmental Labeling and Charter, M. (ed.) 1992. Greener marketing: a responsible approach to business. Sheffield, Greenleaf Publishing 403p.

Chemical Week, 1999. Europe's Beef Ban Tests Precautionary Principle. (August 11).

CHOI, J.P. Brand Extension as Informational Leverage. Review of Eco- nomic Studies, Vol. 65 (1998), pp. 655-669.

Conway, G. 2000. Genetically modified crops: risks and promise.

Corrado, M., (1989), The Greening Consumer in Britain, MORI, London

Corrado, M., (1997), Green Behaviour – Sustainable Trends, Sustainable Lives?, MORI, london, accessed via countries. Manila, Asian Development Bank 33p.

Cropper, M.L., L.D. Deck, and K.E. McConnell. "On the choice of Functional Forms for Hedonic Price Functions," Review of Economics and Statistics 70(1988): 668-675.

Darbi, M. R. and E. Karni, (1973), Free Competition and the Optimal

Davis, G. 1998. Environmental Labeling Issues, Policies, and Practices Worldwide. Washington, DC. EPA, 216p.

Dawkins, K. 1996. Eco-labeling: consumer's right-to-know or restrictive business practice? Minneapolis, Minn., Institute for Agriculture and Trade Policy.

Di Leva, C. E. 1998. International Environmental Law and Development. Georgetown Interna. Environ. Law Review 10 (2): 502-549.

Economics and Management 43, 339-359.

Eiderstroem, E. 1997. Eco-labeling: Swedish Style. Forum for Applied Research in Public Policy 141(4).

Elkington, J. and Hailes, J. 1990. The green consumer guide: You can buy products that don't cost the earth. New York, Viking Press. 96p.

EMONS, W. Credence Goods and Fraudulent Experts. RAND Journal of Economics, Vol. 28 (1997), pp. 107-119.

EMONS, W. Credence Goods Monopolists. International Journal of In- dustrial Organization, Vol. 19 (2001), pp. 375-389.

Energy.gov, Advantages and Challenges of Wind Energy, Retrieved from: https://www.energy.gov/eere/wind/advantages-and-challenges-wind-energy

Energy.gov, Advantages and Challenges of Wind Energy, Retrieved from: https://www.energy.gov/eere/wind/advantages-and-challenges-wind-energy

Environment Canada 1997. Towards Greener Government Procurement: An Environment Canada Case Study (pp. 31-46). in Greener Purchasing: Opportunities and Innovations.

Environmental Protection Agency 742-R-98-009, (1998),

Environmentalist 17 (2): 125-133.

Erskine, C.C. and Collins, L. 1996. Eco-labeling in the EU: a comparative study of the pulp and paper industry in the UK and Sweden. European Environment 17 (2) : 40-47.

Erskine, C.C. and Collins, L. 1997. "Eco-labeling: Success or failure?".

Ethical Consumer, (1995), Co-op Supermarkets take up Ethics, EC36, June/July, p4

Ethical Consumer, (June 1996), Green Cons, EC41, June, p5

European Communities, Commission of the, 1996. Eco-label revision.

European Communities, Commission of the. 1996. Conservation of West Africa's forests through certification. UN Courier 157: 71-73.

European Union official website: https://ec.europa.eu/info/about-european-commission/contact_en

Feenstra, R.C. "Exact Hedonic Price Indexes," Review of Economics and Statistics 77 (1995): 634-653.

Feenstra, R.C., and J.A. Levinsohn. "Estimating Markups and Market Conduct with Multidimensional Product Attributes," Review of Economic Studies (62 (1995): 19-52.

Forest Stewardship Council: "Principles and criteria for forest stewardship" Document 1.2: <http://www.fscoax.org>

Forsyth, K. 1999. Will consumers pay more for certified wood products? Journal of Forestry 97 (2) : 18-22.

Freeman, A. M III. The Measurement of Environmental and Resource Values. Theory and Methods. Washington D.C.: Resource for the Future, 1993.

Friends of the Earth, 1993. Timber certification and eco-labeling. London, FOE:

Graves, P., J.C. Murdoch, M.A. Thayer, and D. Waldman. "The Robustness of Hedonic Price Estimation: Urban Air Quality," Land Economics 64(1988): 220-233.

Halvorsen, R. and R. Palmquist. "The Interpretation of Dummy Variables in Semilogarithmic Equations." American Economic Review 70:474-75 (1980).

Imhoff, Dan, and Grose, Lynda, and Carra, Roberto., "Organic Cotton Exhibit," Mimeo. Simple Life and distributed the Texas Organic Cotton Marketing Cooperative, O'Donnell, Texas (1996).

Imhoff, Dan. "Growing Pains: Organic Cotton Tests the Fiber of Growers and Manufacturers Alike," reprinted on Simple Life's web page (simplelife.com), but first printed by Farmer to Farmer, December 1995.

Incomplete Consumer Information in Laboratory Markets. Journal of Environmental labeling.

ISO 14020, ISO 14021,ISO 14024,ISO 14025, International Organization for Standardization.

Kennedy, P.E. "Estimation with Correctly Interpreted Dummy Variables in Semilogarithmic Equations," American Economic Review 71: 801 (1981).

Kirchho®, S., (2000), Green Business and Blue Angels.

Kraus, Jeff. Lab Technician at the North Carolina School of Textiles.

Labeling Issues, Policies and Practices Worldwide.

Lamport, L. 1998. The cast of (timber) certifiers: who are they? International J. Ecoforestry 11(4): 118-122.

Large Scale impoverishment of Amazonian forests by logging and fire. 1999.

Lathrop, K.W. and Centner, T.J. 1998. Eco-labeling and ISO 14000: An analysis of US regulatory systems and issues concerning adoption of type II standards. Environmental

Lee, J. et al. 1996. Trade related environmental measures; sizing and comparing impacts.

Lehtonen, Markku. 1997. Criteria in Environmental Labeling: A comparative Analysis on Environmental Criteria in Selected Labeling Schemes. Geneva, UNEP. 148p.

LIEBI, T. Trusting Labels: A Matter of Numbers? Working Paper Uni versity of Bern, No. 0201 (2002).

Lindstrom, T. 1999. Forest Certification: The View from Europe's NIPFs. Journal of Forestry 97(3): 25-31. London

Losey, J.E., Rayor, L.S. & Carter, M.E. 1999. Transgenic pollen harms monarch larvae. Nature 399 20 May): p.214.

Management 22 (2) : 163-172.

Mattoo, A. and H. V. Singh, (1994), Eco-Labelling: Policy Considera-

Michaels, R. G., and V. K. Smith. "Market Segmentation And Valuing Amenities With Hedonic Models: The Case Of Hazardous Waste Sites," Journal of Urban Economics, 1990 28(2), 223-242.

Mintel, (1991), The Green Consumer I, May

Mintel, (1994), The Green Consumer, Mintel Special Report

Moraga-Gonzalez, J. L. and N. Padr¶on-Fumero, (2002),

NCC, (1996a), Green Claims – a consumer investigation into marketing claims about the environment,

NCC, (1996b), Shades of Green – consumers' attitudes to green shopping, National Consumer Council,

Nelson , P."Information and Consumer Behaviour," Journal of Political Economy 78 (1970): 311-329..

Nicholson-Lord, D., (1993) 'Tis the Season to be Green, The Independent, 20 December

Nuttall, N., (1993), Shoppers can cross green products off their lists, The Times, 3 July

OCDE/GD(97)105. Paris, OECD. 81p.

OECD. "Ec-labelling: Actual Effects of Selected Programmes," OCDE/GD (97) 105, 1997, Paris. (available on line at http://www.oecd.org/env/eco/books.htm#trademono)

OECD. 1997a. Case study on eco-labeling schemes. Paris, OECD (30 Dec):

OECD. 1997b. Eco-labeling: Actual Effects of Selected Programs.

Osborne, L. "Market Structure, Hedonic Models, and the Valuation of Environmental Amenities." Unpublished Ph.D. dissertation. North Carolina State University, 1995.

Osborne, L., and V. K. Smith. "Environmental Amenities, Product Differentiation, and market Power," Mimeo, 1997.

Ozanne, L.K. and Vlosky, R.P. 1996. Wood products environmental certification: the United States perspective". Forestry Chronicle 72 (2) : 157-165.

Palmquist, R. B., F. M. Roka, and T.Vukina. "Hog Operations, Environmental Effects, and Residential Property Values," Land Economics 73(1), (1997): 114-24.

Palmquist, R.B. "Hedonic Methods," in J.B Braden and C.D. Kolstad, eds. Measuring the Demand for Environmental Improvement. Amsterdam, NL: Elsevier, 1991.

Pento, T. 1997. Implementation of Public Green Procurement Programs (22-31) in Greener Purchasing: Opportunities and Innovations. Sheffield, Greenleaf Publ. 325 p.

Perloff, J. "Industrial Organization Lecture Notes," Mimeo. University of California at Berkeley (1985).

Plant, C. and Plant, J. 1991. Green business: hope or hoax? Philadelphia, New Society Publishers 136 p.

Polak, J. and Bergholm, K. 1997. Eco-labeling and trade: a cooperative approach (Jan.): Policy in a Green Market. Environmental and Resource Economics 22, 419-

Poore, M.E.D. et al. 1989. No timber without trees. London, Earthscan. 352p.

Raff, D. M.G., and M. Trajtenberg. "Quality-Adjusted Prices for the American Automobile Industry: 1906-1940." NBER Working Paper Series, Working Paper No. 5035, February 1995.

Rastogi, J. 1998. What's Behind the Label? Complexities of Certified Wood. Ecoforestry 13 (2): 38-42.

Roberts, J. T. 1998. Emerging global environment standards: prospects and perils. Journal of Developing Societies 14 (1): 144-163.

Rosen, S., "Hedonic Prices and Implicit Markets: Product Differentiation in Pure Competition." Journal of Political Economy. 82: 34-55 (1974).

Ross, B. 1997. Eco-friendly procurement training course for UN HCR. : 126 p.

Ryan, S., and Skipworth, M., (1993), Consumers turn their backs on green revolution, The Times, 4 April

Salzman, J. 1997. Informing the Green Consumer: The Debate over the Use and Abuse of Environmental Labels. Journal of Industrial Ecology 1 (2): 11-22.

Sanders, W. 1997. Environmentally Preferable Purchasing: The US Experience (946-960) in Greener Purchasing: Opportunities and Innovations. Sheffield, Greenleaf Publ. 325p.

Sayre, D. 1996. Inside ISO 14000: The competitive advantage of environmental management. Delray Beach FL., St. Lucie Press. 232p.

SHAPIRO, C. Premiums for High Quality Products as Returns to Reputa- tion. Quarterly Journal of Economics, Vol. 98, No. 4 (1983), pp. 659-680.

Stillwell, M. and van Dyke, B. 1999. An activists handbook on genetically modified organisms and the WTO. Washington DC., The Consumer's Choice Council: 20 p.

Teisl, M. F., B. Roe, and R. L. Hicks. "Can Eco-labels tune a market? Evidence from dolphin-safe labeling," Presented paper at the 1997 American Agricultural Economics Association Meetings, Toronto.

THE GERSEN, C. Psychological Determinants of Paying Attention to Eco- Labels in Purchase Decisions: Model Development and Multinational Vali- dation. Journal of Consumer Policy, Vol. 23, No. 4 (2000), pp. 285-313.

Tibor, T. and Feldman, I. 1995. ISO 14000: a guide to the new environmental management standards. Burr Ridge Ill., Irwin Professional Publ. 250 p.

Torre, I. de la, & Batker, D. K. (n.d.) 1999-2000. Prawn to trade: prawn to consume. Graham WA., Industrial Shrimp Action Network (isatorre@seanet.com), [and] Asia –Pacific Townsend, M. 1998. Making things greener: motivations and influences in the greening of manufacturing. Aldershot, England, Ashgate Publisher. 203p.

U.S. Energy Information Administration, What is U.S. Electricity Generation by Energy Source?, Retrieved From: https://www.eia.gov/tools/faqs/faq.php?id=427&t=3

U.S. Energy Information Administration, Biomass Explained, Retrieved From: https://www.eia.gov/energyexplained/?page=biomass_home

U.S. Environmental Protection Agency. National Water Quality Fact Inventory: 1990 Report to Congress. EPA 503-9-92-006, Apr. 1992.

UK Eco-labelling Board website, accessed via http://www.ecosite.co.uk/Ecolabel-UK/

US Environmental Protection Agency (EPA742-R-99-001): 40 p. <www.epa.gov/opptintr/epp>

US EPA, 1993. Determinants of effectiveness for environmental certification and labeling programs. Washington, D.C., US Environmental Protect

US EPA, 1993. Status report on the use of environmental labels worldwide. Washington, D.C., US Environmental Protection Agency (742-R-93-001 September).

US EPA, 1993. The use of life-cycle assessment in environmental labeling. Washington, D.C., US Environmental Protection Agency (742-R-93-003 September).

US EPA, 1998. Environmental labeling: issues, policies, and practices worldwide. Washington DC., Environmental Protection Agency, Pollution Prevention Division Prepared by Abt

US EPA, 1999. Comprehensive procurement guidelines (CPG) program. Washington, D.C., US Environmental Protection Agency: <www.epa.gov/cpg>

US EPA, 1999. Environmentally preferable purchasing program: Private sector pioneers: How companies are incorporating environmentally preferable purchases. Washington, D.C.,

USG, 1993. Federal acquisition, recycling, and waste prevention. Washington DC., Executive Order: (20 October).

USG, 1998. Greening the government through waste prevention, recycling, and federal acquisition. Washington, D.C., Executive Order 13101 (September).

Van der Grijp, N. 1998. The Greening of Public Procurement in the Netherlands (60-71) in Greener Purchasing: Opportunities and Innovations. Sheffield, Greenleaf Pub. 325 p.

Vanclay, J.K. 1996. Lessons from the Queensland rainforests: steps towards sustainability. J. Sustainable Forestry 3 (2/3): 1-25.

Vidal, J., (1993), Shopping for a paler shade of green, The Guardian, 7 April

Voluntary Overcompliance. Journal of Economic Behavior and Organization

Von Felbert, D. 1995. Trade, environment and aid. Paris, OECD Observer 195: 6-10.

Ward, H. 1997. Review of European Community and International Environmental Law 6 (2): 139-147.

Wasik, John, F. Green Marketing and Management: a Global Perspective, Blackwell Business: Cambridge, Mass, 1996.

West, K. 1995. Ecolabels: the industrialization of environmental standards. The Ecologist (Jan/Feb) 25: 16-20.

Worcester, R., (1995), Business and the Environment – in the aftermath of Brent Spar and BSE, MORI,

World Commission on Forests and Sustainable Development: Final Report. <http://iisd.ca/wcfsd>.

Zarrilli, S., V. Jha, and R. Vossenaar, eds. Eco-labelling and International Trade, St martin Press, Inc. New-York, 1997.

Environmental Lifestyle Guide

For Grade 9

For Grade 10

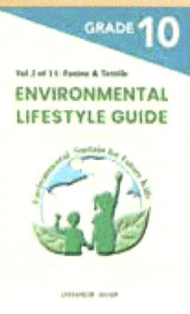  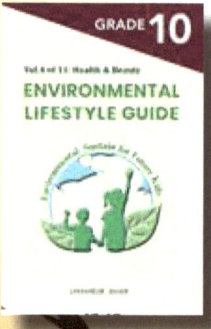

Plus Online Certification Tests via:
https://toptenaward.org

Standard Text Books

For Grade 11

For Grade 12

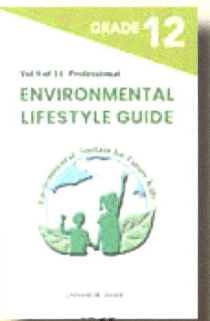 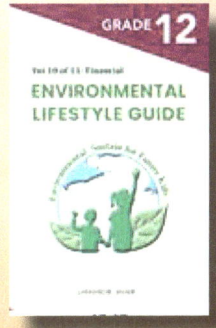 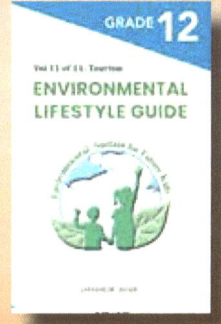

**Environmental Lifestyle Guide
Standard Text Book**
For Students Grade 9 to 12
Available in more than
39,000 Bookstores
all over the globe.
https://ecofriendlyeducation.com

**Cooperation by:
Top Ten Award International Network
&
Environmental Sustain for Future Kids**

www.ingramcontent.com/pod-product-compliance
Lightning Source LLC
Chambersburg PA
CBHW040859120626
46551CB00001B/79